Words From
THE GARDEN

A collection of beautiful
poetry, prose and quotations

Isobel Carlson

summersdale

WORDS FROM THE GARDEN

First published in 2008
This edition copyright Summersdale Publishers Ltd, 2014

Summersdale Publishers Ltd
46 West Street
Chichester
West Sussex
PO19 1RP
UK

www.summersdale.com

Printed and bound in the Czech Republic

ISBN: 978-1-84953-529-8

Substantial discounts on bulk quantities of Summersdale books are available to corporations, professional associations and other organisations. For details contact Nicky Douglas by telephone: +44 (0) 1243 756902, fax: +44 (0) 1243 786300 or email: nicky@summersdale.com.

TO.....................................

FROM.............................

A modest garden contains, for those who know how to look and to wait, more instruction than a library.

Henri Frédéric Amiel

Garden Thoughts

The kiss of the sun for pardon,
The song of the birds for mirth,
One is nearer God's heart in a garden
Than anywhere else on earth.

Dorothy Frances Gurney

Let us, then, begin by defining what a garden is, and what it ought to be. It is a piece of ground fenced off from cattle, and appropriated to the use and pleasure of man: it is or ought to be, cultivated and enriched by art, with such products as are not natural to this country, and, consequently, it must be artificial in its treatment, and may, without impropriety, be so in its appearance; yet, there is so much of littleness in art, when compared with nature, that they cannot well be blended; it were, therefore, to be wished, that the exterior of a garden should be made to assimilate with park scenery, or the landscape of nature; the interior may then be laid out with all the variety, contrast, and even whim, that can produce pleasing objects to the eye.

Humphry Repton, *Observations on the Theory and Practice of Landscape Gardening*

The Barry garden was a bowery wilderness of flowers which would have delighted Anne's heart at any time less fraught with destiny. It was encircled by huge old willows and tall firs, beneath which flourished flowers that loved the shade. Prim, right-angled paths, neatly bordered with clamshells, intersected it like moist red ribbons and in the beds between old-fashioned flowers ran riot. There were rosy bleeding-hearts and great splendid crimson peonies; white, fragrant narcissi and thorny, sweet Scotch roses; pink and blue and white columbines and lilac-tinted Bouncing Bets; clumps of southernwood and ribbon grass and mint; purple Adam-and-Eve, daffodils, and masses of sweet clover white with its delicate, fragrant, feathery sprays; scarlet lightning that shot its fiery lances over prim white musk-flowers; a garden it was where sunshine lingered and bees hummed, and winds, beguiled into loitering, purred and rustled.

L. M. Montgomery, *Anne of Green Gables*

The Caterpillar

Brown and furry
Caterpillar in a hurry,
Take your walk
To the shady leaf, or stalk,
Or what not,
Which may be the chosen spot.
No toad spy you,
Hovering bird of prey pass by you:
Spin and die,
To live again a butterfly.

Christina Rossetti

from The Feat of Gardening

How so well a gardener be,
Here he may both hear and see
Every time of the year and of the moon
And how the crafte shall be done,
In what manner he shall delve and set
Both in drought and in wet,
How he shall his seeds sow;
Of every month he must know
Both of wortes and of leek,
Onions and of garlic,
Parsley, clary and eke sage
And all other herbage.

John Gardner

Behind a Wall

I own a solace shut within my heart,
A garden full of many a quaint delight
And warm with drowsy, poppied
                    sunshine; bright,
Flaming with lilies out of whose cups dart
            Shining things
            With powdered wings.

Here terrace sinks to terrace, arbors close
The ends of dreaming paths; a wanton wind
Jostles the half-ripe pears, and then, unkind,
      Tumbles a-slumber in a pillar rose,
            With content
            Grown indolent.

By night my garden is o'erhung with gems
   Fixed in an onyx setting. Fireflies
Flicker their lanterns in my dazzled eyes.
In serried rows I guess the straight, stiff stems
      Of hollyhocks
     Against the rocks.

  So far and still it is that, listening,
I hear the flowers talking in the dawn;
And where a sunken basin cuts the lawn,
  Cinctured with iris, pale and glistening,
      The sudden swish
     Of a waking fish.

Amy Lowell

Our 'garden's sacred round' is free to every bird that flies – the delight of seeing them, and of hearing their music, compensates to the full any ravages they may indulge in. Thanks to netting without stint, and our Gardener's incomparable patience and longsuffering, I enjoy the garden and my birds in peace; and if they ever do any harm, we never know it; fruit and green Peas never fail us! ... Here is a sunny morning; and the cows are whisking their tails under the Elms, as if it were July. But indeed the last lingering trace of summer has vanished: the garden is in ruins, and already the redbreast is singing songs of triumph.

Eleanor Vere Boyle,
Days and Hours in a Garden

You have heard it said that flowers only flourish rightly in the garden of someone who loves them. I know you would like that to be true; and would think it a pleasant magic if you could flush your flowers into brighter bloom by a kind look upon them.

John Ruskin, *Sesame and Lilies*

from Magdalen Walks

The little white clouds are racing over
the sky,
And the fields are strewn with the gold of
the flower of March,
The daffodil breaks under foot, and the
tasselled larch
Sways and swings as the thrush goes
hurrying by.

A delicate odour is borne on the wings of
the morning breeze,
The odour of deep wet grass, and of
brown new-furrowed earth,
The birds are singing for joy of the Spring's
glad birth,
Hopping from branch to branch on the
rocking trees.

And all the woods are alive with the
murmur and sound of spring,
And the rose bud breaks into pink on the
climbing briar,
And the crocus-bed is a quivering moon
of fire
Girdled round with the belt of an
amethyst ring.

And the plane to the pine-tree is
whispering some tale of love
Till it rustles with laughter and tosses its
mantle of green,
And the gloom of the wych-elm's hollow is
lit with the iris sheen
Of the burnished rainbow throat and the
silver breast of a dove.

Oscar Wilde

How fair is a garden amid the toils and passions of existence.

Benjamin Disraeli

It was the sweetest, most mysterious-looking place any one could imagine. The high walls which shut it in were covered with the leafless stems of climbing roses, which were so thick that they were matted together. Mary Lennox knew they were roses because she had seen a great many roses in India. All the ground was covered with grass of a wintry brown and out of it grew clumps of bushes which were surely rosebushes if they were alive. There were numbers of standard roses which had so spread their branches that they were like little trees. There were other trees in the garden, and one of the things which made the place look strangest and loveliest was that climbing roses had run all over them and swung down long tendrils which made light swaying curtains, and here and there they had caught at each other or at a far-reaching branch and had crept from one tree to another and made lovely bridges of themselves.

There were neither leaves nor roses on them now and Mary did not know whether they were dead or alive, but their thin grey or brown branches and sprays looked like a sort of hazy mantle spreading over everything, walls, and trees, and even brown grass, where they had fallen from their fastenings and run along the ground. It was this hazy tangle from tree to tree which made it all look so mysterious. Mary had thought it must be different from other gardens which had not been left all by themselves so long; and indeed it was different from any other place she had ever seen in her life.

'How still it is!' she whispered. 'How still!'

Frances Hodgson Burnett,
The Secret Garden

Having commenced gardening, I study the arts of pruning, sowing, and planting; and enterprise every thing in that way, from melons down to cabbages. I have a large garden to display my abilities in, and, were we twenty miles nearer London, I might turn higgler, and serve your honour with cauliflowers, and broccoli, at the best hand. I shall possibly now and then desire you to call at the seed-shop, in your way to Westminster, though sparingly. Should I do it often, you would begin to think you had a mother-in-law at Berkhampstead.

William Cowper to Mrs Cowper, 1767

The Ant Explorer

Once a little sugar ant made up his mind
to roam –
To fare away far away, far away from home.
He had eaten all his breakfast, and he had
his ma's consent
To see what he should chance to see and
here's the way he went –
Up and down a fern frond, round and
round a stone,
Down a gloomy gully, where he loathed to
be alone,
Up a mighty mountain range, seven
inches high,

Through the fearful forest grass that nearly
hid the sky,
Out along a bracken bridge, bending in
the moss,
Till he reached a dreadful desert that was
feet and feet across.
'Twas a dry, deserted desert, and a
trackless land to tread;
He wished that he was home again and
tucked up tight in bed.
His little legs were wobbly, his strength
was nearly spent,
And so he turned around again and here's
the way he went –
Back along a bracken bridge, bending in
the moss,
Through the fearful forest grass shutting
out the sky,

Up a mighty mountain range, seven
inches high,
Down a gloomy gully, where he loathed to
be alone,
Up and down a fern frond, round and
round a stone.
A dreary ant, a weary ant, resolved no
more to roam,
He staggered up the garden path and
popped back home.

C. J. Dennis

They reached the flower-garden, and turned mechanically in at the gate that opened, through a high thick hedge, on an expanse of brilliant colour, which, after the green shades they had passed through, startled the eye like flames... the flowers were glowing with their evening splendours; verbenas and heliotropes were sending up their finest incense. It seemed a gala where all was happiness and brilliancy, and misery could find no sympathy.

George Eliot, *Scenes of Clerical Life*

The Gardener wi' his Paidle

When rosy May comes in wi' flowers
To deck her gay, green, spreading bowers;
 Then busy, busy are his hours,
  The gardener wi' his paidle. –

  The crystal waters gently fa';
  The merry birds are lovers a';
 The scented breezes round him blaw,
  The gardener wi' his paidle. –

When purple morning starts the hare
To steal upon her early fare;
Then thro' the dews he maun repair,
The gardener wi' his paidle. –

When Day, expiring in the west,
The curtain draws of Nature's rest;
He flies to her arms he lo'es the best,
The gardener wi' his paidle. –

Robert Burns

He rambled an hour in breathless ecstasy, brushing the dew from the deep fern and bracken and the rich borders of the garden, tasting the fragrant air and stopping everywhere in murmuring rapture, at the touch of some exquisite impression. His whole walk was peopled with recognitions; he had been dreaming all his life of just such a place and such objects, such a morning and such a chance. It was the last of April and everything was fresh and vivid; the great trees, in the early air, were a blur of tender shoots. Round the admirable house he revolved repeatedly, catching every aspect and feeling every value, feasting on the whole expression... There was something in the way the grey walls rose from the green lawn that brought tears to his eyes...

Henry James, *The Princess Casamassima*

from The Garden

Bees, humming with soft sound, (their
murmur is so small),
Of blooms and blossoms suck the tops, on
dewed leaves they fall
The creeping vine holds down her own
bewedded elms:
And, wandering out with branches thick,
reeds folded overwhelms.
Trees spread their coverts wide, with
shadows fresh and gay:
Full well their branched boughs defend the
fervent sun away.
Birds chatter, and some chirp, and some
sweet tunes do yield:
All mirthful, with their songs so blithe,
they make both air and field.

The garden it allures, it feeds, it glads
the spirit:
From heavy hearts all doleful dumps the
garden chaseth quite.
Strength it restores to limbs, draws, and
fulfills the sight;
with cheer revives the senses all, and
maketh labour light.
O, what delights to us the garden ground
doth bring?
Seed, leaf, flower, fruit, herb, bee, and tree
and more than I may sing.

Nicholas Grimald

'O Tiger-lily,' said Alice, addressing herself to one that was waving gracefully about in the wind, 'I *wish* you could talk!' 'We *can* talk,' said the Tiger-lily, 'when there's anybody worth talking to.' Alice was so astonished that she couldn't speak for a minute: it quite seemed to take her breath away. At length, as the Tiger-lily only went on waving about, she spoke again, in a timid voice – almost in a whisper. 'And can *all* the flowers talk?' 'As well as *you* can,' said the Tiger-lily. 'And a great deal louder.' 'It isn't manners for us to begin, you know,' said the Rose, 'and I really was wondering when you'd speak! Said I to myself, "Her face has got *some* sense in it, though it's not a clever one!" Still, you're the right colour, and that goes a long way.'

'I don't care about the colour,' the Tiger-lily remarked. 'If only her petals curled up a little more, she'd be all right.' Alice didn't like being criticised, so she began asking questions. 'Aren't you sometimes frightened at being planted out here, with nobody to take care of you?' 'There's the tree in the middle,' said the Rose. 'What else is it good for?'

Lewis Carroll, *Through the Looking-Glass*

The many great gardens of the world, of literature and poetry, of painting and music, of religion and architecture, all make the point as clear as possible: The soul cannot thrive in the absence of a garden...

Thomas Moore

While such honey-dew fell, such silence reigned, such gloaming gathered, I felt as if I could haunt such shade for ever: but in threading the flower and fruit-parterres at the upper part of the inclosure, enticed there by the light the now-risen moon casts on this more open quarter, my step is stayed – not by sound, not by sight, but once more by a warning fragrance. Sweet briar and southernwood, jasmine, pink, and rose, have long been yielding their evening sacrifice of incense: this new scent is neither of shrub nor flower; it is – I know it well – it is Mr Rochester's cigar.

Charlotte Brontë, *Jane Eyre*

Robin

The sparrow seeks his feathers for a nest
And the fond robin with his ruddy breast
Hops round the garden wall where
thickly twine
The leafing sweet briar and the
propt woodbine
And in a hole behind the thickening boughs
He builds with hopeful joy his little house
Stealing with jealous speed the wool and hair
Where cows and sheep have lain them
down to lair
And pecks the green moss in his
murmuring glee
From cottage thatch and squatting apple tree
Tutling his song –

John Clare

A gap in the hedge gave a view into the gardens; a border of jasmine, pansies and verbena which ran along the wide path, was interplanted with fragrant wallflowers the faded rose of old Cordoba leather. A long green hose snaking across the gravel sent up every few yards a vertical, prismatic fan, and the multicoloured drops showered over the flowers in a perfumed cloud.

Marcel Proust, *Swann's Way*

What a desolate place would be a world without a flower! It would be a face without a smile, a feast without a welcome.

A. J. Balfour

In fine weather the old gentleman is almost constantly in the garden, and when it is too wet to go into it, he will look out of the window at it, by the hour together. He has always something to do there, and you will see him digging, and sweeping, and cutting, and planting, with manifest delight. In spring-time there is no end to the sowing of seeds, and sticking little bits of wood over them, with labels, which look like epitaphs to their memory; and in the evening, when the sun has gone down, the perseverance with which he lugs a great watering-pot about is perfectly astonishing...

Charles Dickens, *Sketches by Boz*

from Leaves of Grass

Give me the splendid silent sun, with all
his beams full-dazzling;
Give me juicy autumnal fruit, ripe and red
from the orchard;
Give me a field where the unmow'd
grass grows;
Give me an arbor, give me the trellis'd grape;
Give me fresh corn and wheat – give me
serene-moving animals, teaching content;
Give me nights perfectly quiet, as on high
plateaus west of the Mississippi, and I
looking up at the stars;
Give me odorous at sunrise a garden of

beautiful flowers, where I can
walk undisturb'd;
Give me for marriage a sweet-breath'd
woman, of whom I should never tire;
Give me a perfect child – give me, away,
aside from the noise of the world, a rural
domestic life;
Give me to warble spontaneous songs,
reliev'd, recluse by myself, for my own
ears only;
Give me solitude – give me Nature – give
me again,
O Nature, your primal sanities!

Walt Whitman

It might once have been the pleasure-place of an opulent family; for there was the ruin of a marble fountain in the centre, sculptured with rare art, but so wofully shattered that it was impossible to trace the original design from the chaos of remaining fragments. The water, however, continued to gush and sparkle into the sunbeams as cheerfully as ever. A little gurgling sound ascended to the young man's window, and made him feel as if the fountain were an immortal spirit that sung its song unceasingly and without heeding the vicissitudes around it, while one century embodied it in marble and another scattered the perishable garniture on the soil. All about the pool into which the water subsided grew various plants, that seemed to require a plentiful supply of moisture for the nourishment of gigantic leaves, and in some instances, flowers gorgeously magnificent. There was one shrub in particular, set in a marble vase in the midst of the pool, that bore a profusion of purple blossoms, each of which had the lustre and richness of a gem; and the whole together made a show so resplendent that it seemed enough to illuminate the garden, even had there been no sunshine. Every portion of the soil was peopled with plants and herbs, which, if less beautiful, still bore tokens of assiduous care, as if all had their individual virtues, known to the scientific mind that fostered them. Some were placed in urns, rich with old carving, and others in common garden pots; some crept serpent-like along the ground or climbed on high, using whatever means of ascent was offered them. One plant had wreathed itself round a statue of Vertumnus, which was thus quite veiled and shrouded in a drapery of hanging foliage, so happily arranged that it might have served a sculptor for a study.

Nathaniel Hawthorne,
'Rappaccini's Daughter'

The Lily

The modest Rose puts forth a thorn,
The humble Sheep a threat'ning horn;
While the Lily white shall in love delight,
Nor a thorn, nor a threat, stain her
beauty bright.

William Blake

The moonbeam fell upon the roof and garden of Gerard. It suffused the cottage with its brilliant light, except where the dark depth of the embowered porch defied its entry. All around the beds of flowers and herbs spread sparkling and defined. You could trace the minutest walk; almost distinguish every leaf. Now and then there came a breath, and the sweet-peas murmured in their sleep; or the roses rustled, as if they were afraid they were about to be roused from their lightsome dreams. Farther on the fruit trees caught the splendour of the night; and looked like a troop of sultanas taking their garden air, when the eye of man could not prophane them, and laden with jewels. There were apples that rivalled rubies; pears of topaz tint; a whole paraphernalia of plums, some purple as the amethyst, others blue and brilliant as the sapphire; an emerald here, and now a golden drop that gleamed like the yellow diamond of Gengis Khan.

Benjamin Disraeli, *Sybil*

from Upon Appleton House

See how the flowers, as at parade,
Under their colours stand displayed;
Each regiment in order grows,
That of the tulip, pink, and rose.
But when the vigilant patrol
Of stars walks round about the pole,
Their leaves that to the stalks are curled
Seem to their staves the ensigns furled.
Then in some flower's belovèd hut,
Each bee, as sentinel, is shut,
And sleeps so too, but, if once stirred,
She runs you through, nor asks the word.

Andrew Marvell

It seems to me (but I believe it seems so every year) that our trees keep their leaves very long; I suppose, because of no severe frosts or winds up to this time. And my garden still shows some Geranium, Salvia, Nasturtium, Great Convolvulus, and that grand African Marigold whose Colour is so comfortable to us Spanish-like Paddies. I have also a dear Oleander which even now has a score of blossoms on it, and touches the top of my little Green-house; having been sent me when 'haut comme ça,' as Marquis Somebody used to say in the days of Louis XIV. Don't you love the Oleander? So clean in its leaves and stem, as so beautiful in its flower; loving to stand in water which it drinks up so fast. I rather worship mine.

Edward Fitzgerald to Mrs Kemble, 1882

The Months

January brings the snow,
Makes our feet and fingers glow.

February brings the rain,
Thaws the frozen lake again.

March brings breezes loud and shrill,
Stirs the dancing daffodil.

April brings the primrose sweet,
Scatters daisies at our feet.

May brings flocks of pretty lambs,
Skipping by their fleecy dams.

June brings tulips, lilies, roses,
Fills the children's hands with posies.

Hot July brings cooling showers,
Apricots and gillyflowers.

August brings the sheaves of corn,
Then the harvest home is borne.

Warm September brings the fruit,
Sportsmen then begin to shoot.

Fresh October brings the pheasant,
Then to gather nuts is pleasant.

Dull November brings the blast,
Then the leaves are whirling fast.

Chill December brings the sleet,
Blazing fire, and Christmas treat.

Sara Coleridge

This is a most beautiful day of English winter; clear and bright, with the ground a little frozen, and the green grass along the waysides at Rock Ferry sprouting up through the frozen pools of yesterday's rain. England is forever green. On Christmas day, the children found wall-flowers, pansies, and pinks in the garden; and we had a beautiful rose from the garden of the hotel grown in the open air.

Nathaniel Hawthorne, *Passages from the English Note-Books of Nathaniel Hawthorne*

Written at a Farm

Around my porch and lowly casement spread;
  The myrtle never-sear, and gadding vine,
With fragrant sweet-briar love to intertwine;
  And in my garden's box-encircled bed,
The pansy pied, and musk-rose white and red,
The pink and tulip, and honeyed woodbine,
Fling odours round; the flaunting eglantine
  Decks my trim fence, 'neath which, by
            silence led,

The wren hath wisely placed her mossy cell;
And far from noise, in courtly land so rife,
Nestles her young to rest, and warbles well.
Here in this safe retreat and peaceful glen
I pass my sober moments, far from men;
Nor wishing death too soon, nor asking life.

John Codrington Bampfylde

A Garden Song

Here in this sequestered close
Bloom the hyacinth and rose,
Here beside the modest stock
Flaunts the flaring hollyhock;
Here, without a pang, one sees
Ranks, conditions, and degrees.

All the seasons run their race
In this quiet resting place,
Peach and apricot and fig
Here will ripen and grow big;
Here is store and overplus,
More had not Alcinoüs!

Here, in alleys cool and green,
Far ahead the thrush is seen;
Here along the southern wall
Keeps the bee his festival;
All is quiet else – afar
Sounds of toil and turmoil are.

Here be shadows large and long;
Here be spaces meet for song;
Grant, O garden-god, that I,
Now that none profane is nigh,
Now that mood and moment please,
Find the fair Pierides!

Henry Austin Dobson

I value my garden more for being full of blackbirds than of cherries, and very frankly give them fruit for their songs.

Joseph Addison

A lovely warm sunny morning, the purple plumes of the silver birch fast thickening with buds waved and swayed gently in the soft spring air against the deep cloudless blue sky. The apricot blossoms were blowing and under the silver weeping birch the daffodils were dancing and nodding their golden heads in the morning wind and sunshine.

Rev. Francis Kilvert

To Blossoms

Why do you fall so fast?
Your date is not so past,
But you may stay yet here awhile,
To blush and gently smile,
And go at last.

What! were ye born to be
An hour or half's delight,
And so to bid good night?
'Tis pity nature brought ye forth
Merely to show your worth,
And lose you quite.

But you are lovely leaves, where we
May read how soon things have
Their end, though ne'er so brave:
And after they have shown their pride,
Like you awhile, they glide
Into the grave.

Robert Herrick

Here at Manderley a new day was starting, the things of the garden were not concerned with our troubles.

Daphne du Maurier, *Rebecca*

The pride of my heart and the delight of my eyes is my garden... I know nothing so pleasant as to sit there on a summer afternoon, with the western sun flickering through the great elder-tree, and lighting up our gay parterres, where flowers and flowering shrubs are set as thick as grass in a field, a wilderness of blossom, interwoven, intertwined, wreathy, garlandy, profuse beyond all profusion, where we may guess that there is such a thing as mould, but never see it. I know nothing so pleasant as to sit in the shade of that dark bower, with the eye resting on that bright piece of colour, lighted so gloriously by the evening sun...

Mary Mitford, *Our Village*

Digging

Today I think
Only with scents, – scents dead leaves yield,
And bracken, and wild carrot's seed,
And the square mustard field;

Odours that rise
When the spade wounds the root of tree,
Rose, currant, raspberry, or goutweed,
Rhubarb or celery;

The smoke's smell, too,
Flowing from where a bonfire burns
The dead, the waste, the dangerous,
And all to sweetness turns.

It is enough
To smell, to crumble the dark earth,
While the robin sings over again
Sad songs of Autumn mirth.

Edward Thomas

Ivy grows so lavishly here that it has to be kept well in hand, and many whom it favours less, have said they envied us our Ivy. More than once we have had to choose between some tree, or a canopy of Ivy. It is like a beautiful carpet underneath a long row of Elms, where nothing else would grow; indeed, wherever there happen to be bits too overshadowed for grass or otherwise unsatisfactory, we put in Ivy; it is sure to understand, and to do what is required. My favourite sort is the wild English Ivy, and no other has a right to grow on the House. Its growth is slow and sure; it always grows to beauty, and never to over-richness. The loveliness of its younger shoots and of the deeply cut leaves might inspire either poet or painter! To either I would say, wherever on your tree, or fence, or house-wall, you find it beginning to spring, cherish it; for years it will do no harm, and if you are true to your art, and therefore know that small things are not too small for you, it will repay your love a hundredfold.

Eleanor Vere Boyle,
Days and Hours in a Garden

from Ah! Sun-flower!

Ah, Sun-flower! weary of time,
Who countest the steps of the Sun:
Seeking after that sweet golden clime,
Where the traveller's journey is done.

William Blake

If well managed, nothing is more beautiful than the kitchen garden: the earliest blossoms come there: we shall in vain seek for flowering shrubs in March, and early in April, to equal the peaches, nectarines, apricots and plums; late in April, we shall find nothing to equal the pear and the cherry; and, in May, the dwarf, or espalier, apple-trees, are just so many immense garlands of carnations.

William Cobbett,
The English Gardener

from The Garden

Fair Quiet, have I found thee here,
And Innocence, thy sister dear!
Mistaken long, I sought you then
In busy companies of men;
Your sacred plants, if here below,
Only among the plants will grow.
Society is all but rude,
To this delicious solitude.

No white nor red was ever seen
So am'rous as this lovely green.
Fond lovers, cruel as their flame,
Cut in these trees their mistress' name;
Little, alas, they know or heed
How far these beauties hers exceed!
Fair trees! Wheres'e'er your barks I wound,
No name shall but your own be found.

Here at the fountain's sliding foot,
Or at some fruit tree's mossy root,
Casting the body's vest aside,
My soul into the boughs does glide;
There like a bird it sits and sings,
Then whets, and combs its silver wings;
And, till prepar'd for longer flight,
Waves in its plumes the various light.

Such was that happy garden-state,
While man there walk'd without a mate;
After a place so pure and sweet,
What other help could yet be meet!
But 'twas beyond a mortal's share
To wander solitary there:
Two paradises 'twere in one
To live in paradise alone.

How well the skillful gard'ner drew
Of flow'rs and herbs this dial new,
Where from above the milder sun
Does through a fragrant zodiac run;
And as it works, th' industrious bee
Computes its time as well as we.
How could such sweet and
wholesome hours
Be reckon'd but with herbs and flow'rs!

Andrew Marvell

Gardens and flowers have a way of bringing people together, drawing them from their homes.

Clare Ansberry,
The Women of Troy Hill

Now I am in the garden at the back... – a very preserve of butterflies, as I remember it, with a high fence, and a gate and padlock; where the fruit clusters on the trees, riper and richer than fruit has ever been since, in any other garden, and where my mother gathers some in a basket, while I stand by, bolting furtive gooseberries, and trying to look unmoved.

Charles Dickens, *David Copperfield*

I know that if odour were visible, as colour is, I'd see the summer garden in rainbow clouds.

Robert Bridges,
'The Testament of Beauty'

The Gardener

The gardener does not love to talk,
He makes me keep the gravel walk;
And when he puts his tools away,
He locks the door and takes the key.

Away behind the currant row
Where no one else but cook may go,
Far in the plots, I see him dig,
Old and serious, brown and big.

He digs the flowers, green, red, and blue,
Nor wishes to be spoken to.
He digs the flowers and cuts the hay,
And never seems to want to play.

Silly gardener! summer goes,
And winter comes with pinching toes,
When in the garden bare and brown
You must lay your barrow down.

Well now, and while the summer stays,
To profit by these garden days,
O how much wiser you would be
To play at Indian wars with me!

Robert Louis Stevenson

The garden is best to be square; encompassed, on all the four sides, with a stately arched hedge. The arches to be upon pillars of carpenter's work, of some ten foot high and six foot broad; and the spaces between of the same dimension with the breadth of the arch. Over the arches let there be an entire hedge, of some four foot high, framed also upon carpenter's work; and upon the upper hedge, over every arch, a little turret, with a belly, enough to receive a cage of birds; and over every space between the arches some other little figure, with broad plates of round coloured glass, gilt, for the sun to play upon. But this hedge I intend to be raised upon a bank, not steep, but gently slope, of some six foot, set all with flowers. Also I understand that this square of the garden should not be the whole breadth of the ground, but to leave, on either side, ground enough for diversity of side alleys; unto which the two covert alleys of the green may deliver you. But there must be no alleys with hedges at either end of this great enclosure: not at the hither end, for letting your prospect upon this fair hedge from the green; nor at the further end, for letting your prospect from the hedge, through the arches, upon the heath.

Sir Francis Bacon, 'Of Gardens'

The Garden by Moonlight

A black cat among roses,
Phlox, lilac-misted under a
first-quarter moon,
The sweet smells of heliotrope and
night-scented stock.
The garden is very still,
It is dazed with moonlight,
Contented with perfume,
Dreaming the opium dreams of its
folded poppies.
Firefly lights open and vanish
High as the tip buds of the golden glow
Low as the sweet alyssum flowers at my feet.
Moon-shimmer on leaves and trellises,

Moon-spikes shafting through the
snowball bush.
Only the little faces of the ladies' delight
are alert and staring,
Only the cat, padding between the roses,
Shakes a branch and breaks the chequered
pattern
As water is broken by the falling of a leaf.
Then you come,
And you are quiet like the garden,
And white like the alyssum flowers,
And beautiful as the silent sparks of the
fireflies.
Ah, Beloved, do you see those orange lilies?
They knew my mother,
But who belonging to me will they know
When I am gone?

Amy Lowell

It was a still warm day of late summer, but a diviner radiance lay over garden field, and wood for me...

After breakfast I went out to the garden – the flowers seemed to smile and nod their heads at me, leaning with a kind of tender brilliance to greet me; in a thick bush I heard the flute-notes of my favourite thrush – the brisk chirruping of the sparrows came from the ivied gable.

A. C. Benson, 1900

Each sunflower stands with half-transparent shadow sharp cut on the wall behind it; its petals fresh gilt, its centre sparkling with dew.

Eleanor Vere Boyle,
Days and Hours in a Garden

Once more we are back in the month when the robin sings so much. The robins, I find, are the tamest of all the birds in the garden; and as we fork over the beds, or dig new ones, they follow us all about, enjoying much the newly turned-up earth.

Mrs C. W. Earle,
Pot-Pourri from a Surrey Garden

from The Garden in September

Now thin mists temper the slow-ripening
beams
Of the September sun: his golden gleams
On gaudy flowers shine, that prank
the rows
Of high-grown hollyhocks, and all tall shows
That Autumn flaunteth in his bushy bowers;
Where tomtits, hanging from the
drooping heads
Of giant sunflowers, peck the nutty seeds;
And in the feathery aster bees on wing
Seize and set free the honied flowers,
Till thousand stars leap with their visiting:
While ever across the path mazily flit,

Unpiloted in the sun,
The dreamy butterflies
With dazzling colours powdered and
soft glooms,
White, black and crimson stripes, and
peacock eyes,
Or on chance flowers sit,
With idle effort plundering one by one
The nectaries of deepest-throated blooms.

With gentle flaws the western breeze
Into the garden saileth,
Scarce here and there stirring the
single trees,
For his sharpness he vaileth:
So long a comrade of the bearded corn,
Now from the stubbles whence the shocks
are borne,

O'er dewy lawns he turns to stray,
As mindful of the kisses and soft play
Wherewith he enamoured the
light-hearted May,
Ere he deserted her;
Lover of fragrance, and too late repents;
Nor more of heavy hyacinth now
may drink,
Nor spicy pink,
Nor summer's rose, nor garnered lavender,
But the few lingering scents
Of streaked pea, and gillyflower, and stocks
Of courtly purple, and aromatic phlox.

Robert Bridges

There was something in the very air of it that exhilarated, that gave one a sense of lightness and good happening and well being; there was something in the sight of it that made all its colour clean and perfect and subtly luminous. In the instant of coming into it one was exquisitely glad – as only in rare moments and when one is young and joyful one can be glad in this world. And everything was beautiful there…

H. G. Wells, *The Door in the Wall*

A garden isn't meant to be useful. It's for joy.

Rumer Godden

from The Deserted Garden

I mind me in the days departed,
How often underneath the sun
With childish bounds I used to run
To a garden long deserted.

The beds and walks were vanish'd quite;
And wheresoe'er had struck the spade,
The greenest grasses Nature laid,
To sanctify her right.

I call'd the place my wilderness,
For no one enter'd there but I.
The sheep look'd in, the grass to espy,
And pass'd it ne'ertheless.

The trees were interwoven wild,
And spread their boughs enough about
To keep both sheep and shepherd out,
But not a happy child.

Adventurous joy it was for me!
I crept beneath the boughs, and found
A circle smooth of mossy ground
Beneath a poplar-tree.

Old garden rose-trees hedged it in,
Bedropt with roses waxen-white,
Well satisfied with dew and light,
And careless to be seen.

Long years ago, it might befall,
When all the garden flowers were trim,
The grave old gardener prided him
On these the most of all.

[...]

And gladdest hours for me did glide
In silence at the rose-tree wall:
A thrush made gladness musical
Upon the other side.

Nor he nor I did e'er incline
To peck or pluck the blossoms white: –
How should I know but that they might
Lead lives as glad as mine?

Elizabeth Barrett Browning

The patch of land he had made into a garden was famous in the town for the beauty of the flowers which he grew there... By dint of hard work, constant care, and endless buckets of water, he had even become a creator, inventing certain tulips and dahlias which seemed to have been forgotten by nature.

Victor Hugo, *Les Misérables*

What Is Pink?

What is pink? A rose is pink
By the fountain's brink.

What is red? A poppy's red
In its barley bed.

What is blue? The sky is blue
Where the clouds float through.

What is white? A swan is white
Sailing in the light.

What is yellow? Pears are yellow,
    Rich and ripe and mellow.

What is green? The grass is green
    With small flowers between.

What is violet? Clouds are violet
    In the summer twilight.

What is orange? Why, an orange,
    Just an orange!

Christina Rossetti

The garden was a large one, and tastefully laid out; besides several splendid dahlias, there were some other fine flowers still in bloom: but my companion would not give me time to examine them: I must go with him, across the wet grass, to a remote sequestered corner, the most important place in the grounds, because it contained his garden. There were two round beds, stocked with a variety of plants. In one there was a pretty little rose-tree. I paused to admire its lovely blossoms.

Anne Brontë, *Agnes Grey*

It is a greater act of faith to plant a bulb than to plant a tree... to see in these wizened, colourless shapes the subtle curves of the iris reticulata or the tight locks of the hyacinth.

Claire Leighton, *Four Hedges*

from The Kitten and the Falling Leaves

See the kitten on the wall,
Sporting with the leaves that fall,
Withered leaves – one, two, and three –
From the lofty elder tree!
Through the calm and frosty air
Of this morning bright and fair,
Eddying round and round they sink
Softly, slowly: one might think
From the motions that are made,
Every little leaf conveyed
Sylph or faery hither tending,

To this lower world descending,
    Each invisible and mute,
    In his wavering parachute.
– But the kitten, how she starts,
Crouches, stretches, paws, and darts!
First at one, and then its fellow,
Just as light and just as yellow;
There are many now – now one –
Now they stop; and there are none.

William Wordsworth

'Take me into the garden, my boy,' he said at last. 'And tell me all about it.'

And so they led him in.

The place was a wilderness of autumn gold and purple and violet blue and flaming scarlet and on every side were sheaves of late lilies standing together – lilies which were white or white and ruby. He remembered well when the first of them had been planted that just at this season of the year their late glories should reveal themselves. Late roses climbed and hung and clustered and the sunshine deepening the hue of the yellowing trees made one feel that one stood in an embowered temple of gold. The newcomer stood silent just as the children had done when they came into its grayness. He looked round and round.

'I thought it would be dead,' he said.

'Mary thought so at first,' said Colin. 'But it came alive.'

Frances Hodgson Burnett,
The Secret Garden

My Neighbour's Roses

The roses red upon my neighbour's vine
Are owned by him, but they are also mine.
His was the cost, and his the labour, too,
But mine as well as his the joy, their
loveliness to view.

They bloom for me and are for me as fair
As for the man who gives them all his care.
Thus I am rich, because a good man grew
A rose-clad vine for all his neighbours' view.

I know from this that others plant for me,
And what they own, my joy may also be.
So why be selfish, when so much that's fine
Is grown for you, upon your
neighbour's vine.

Abraham L. Gruber

In the Garden

A bird came down the walk,
He did not know I saw,
He bit an angle worm in halves
And ate the fellow, raw.

And then he drank a dew
From a convenient grass,
And then hopped sidewise to the wall
To let a beetle pass.

He glanced with rapid eyes
That hurried all abroad, –
They looked like frightened beads,
I thought;
He stirred his velvet head

Like one in danger; cautious,
I offered him a crumb,
And he unrolled his feathers
And rowed him softer home

Than oars divide the ocean,
Too silver for a seam,
Or butterflies, off banks of noon,
Leap, plashless, as they swim.

Emily Dickinson

The Daisy

The daisy is a happy flower,
And comes at early spring,
And brings with it the sunny hour
When bees are on the wing.

It brings with it the butterfly,
And early humble-bee;
The polyanthus goldeneye,
And blooming apple-tree;

Hedge-sparrows from the mossy nest
In the old garden hedge,
Where schoolboys, in their idle glee,
Seek pooties as their pledge.

The cow stands browsing all the day
Over the orchard gate,
And eats her bits of sweet old hay
And Goody stands to wait;

Lest what's not eaten the rude wind
May rise and snatch away
Over the neighbour's hedge behind,
Where hungry cattle lay.

John Clare

There are, besides the temper of our climate, two things particular to us, that contribute much to the beauty and elegance of our gardens, which are the gravel of our walks, and the fineness and almost perpetual greenness of our turf. The first is not known anywhere else, which leaves all their dry walks in other countries, very unpleasant and uneasy. The other cannot be found in France or in Holland as we have it, the soil not admitting that fineness of blade in Holland, nor the sun that greenness in France, during most of the summer; nor indeed is it to be found but in the finest of our soils.

Sir William Temple, *Upon the Gardens of Epicurus, or of Gardening in the Year 1685*

My flowers grow up in several parts of the garden in the greatest luxuriancy and profusion... if I meet with any one in a field which pleases me, I give it a place in my garden. By this means, when a stranger walks with me, he is surprised to see large spots of ground covered with ten thousand different colours, and has often singled out flowers he might have met with under a common hedge, in a field, or in a meadow, as some of the greatest beauties of the place... I take in none that do not naturally rejoice in the soil, and am pleased, when I am walking, in a labyrinth of my own raising, not to know whether the next tree I shall meet with is an apple or an oak; an elm or a pear tree.

Joseph Addison, *The Spectator*

A Contemplation upon Flowers

Brave flowers – that I could gallant it
like you,
And be as little vain!
You come abroad, and make a
harmless show,
And to your beds of earth again.
You are not proud: you know your birth:
For your embroider'd garments are
from earth.

You do obey your months and times, but I
Would have it ever Spring:
My fate would know no Winter, never die,
Nor think of such a thing.

O that I could my bed of earth but view
And smile, and look as cheerfully as you!

O teach me to see Death and not to fear,
But rather to take truce!
How often have I seen you at a bier,
And there look fresh and spruce!
You fragrant flowers! then teach me, that
my breath
Like yours may sweeten and perfume
my death.

Henry King

There is no gardening without humility. Nature is constantly sending even its oldest scholars to the bottom of the class for some egregious blunder.

Alfred Austin

This house is just on the edge of the town: a garden on one side skirted by the public road which again is skirted by a row of such Poplars as only the Ouse knows how to rear – and pleasantly they rustle now – and the room in which I write is quite cool and opens into a greenhouse which opens into said garden: and it's all deuced pleasant.

Edward Fitzgerald to Bernard Barton, 1839

How beautiful the whole garden looked at the hour when it should have been night, about ten o'clock, in the strange, weirdly daylight! Beyond the high west line of wall and the trees at the upper end, in the cold clear sky lay level flakes of cloud, fired by a sunset glow.

Eleanor Vere Boyle,
Sylvana's Letters to an Unknown Friend

from Hortulus

Though a life of retreat offers various joys,
None, I think, will compare with the time
one employs
In the study of herbs, or in striving to gain
Some practical knowledge of
nature's domain.
Get a garden! What kind you may get
matters not.

Abbot Walafrid Strabo

The orange-trees, and several plants, full and bright with bloom, basked also in the sun's laughing bounty; they had partaken it the whole day, and now asked water. M. Emanuel had a taste for gardening; he liked to tend and foster plants. I used to think that working amongst shrubs with a spade or a watering-pot soothed his nerves; it was a recreation to which he often had recourse; and now he looked to the orange-trees, the geraniums, the gorgeous cactuses, and revived them all with the refreshment their drought needed.

Charlotte Brontë, *Villette*

'I haven't much time to be fond of anything,' says Sergeant Cuff, 'but when I have a moment's fondness to bestow, most times, Mr Betteredge, the roses get it. I began my life among them in my father's nursery garden, and I shall end my life among them, if I can. Yes. One of these days (please God) I shall retire from catching thieves, and try my hand at growing roses.'

Wilkie Collins, *The Moonstone*

On Pruning

Proud of his well-spread walls, he views
his trees
That meet (no barren interval between)
With pleasure more than ev'n their
fruits afford,
Which, save himself who trains them, none
can feel:
These, therefore, are his own peculiar charge;
No meaner hand may disciple the shoots,
None but his steel approach them. What
is weak,
Distemper'd, or has lost prolific pow'rs,
Impair'd by age, his unrelenting hand
Dooms to the knife: nor does he spare
the soft

And succulent, that feeds its giant growth,
But barren, at th' expence of
neighb'ring twigs
Less ostentatious, and yet studded thick
With hopeful gems. The rest, no portion left
That may disgrace his art, or disappoint
Large expectation, he disposes neat
At measur'd distances, that air and sun,
Admitted freely, may afford their aid,
And ventilate and warm the swelling buds.
Hence summer has her riches, autumn hence,
And hence ev'n winter fills his wither'd hand
With blushing fruits, and plenty, not his own.

William Cowper

Not but that the garden choir sang shrill, and two or three cocks, taunting, far away, lifted up their voices on stilts out of the dawning, crying, 'Cock-a-doodle-doo!'

James Smetham to F. J. S., 1877

A half-moon, dusky gold, was sinking behind the black sycamore at the end of the garden, making the sky dull purple with its glow. Nearer, a dim white fence of lilies went across the garden, and the air all round seemed to stir with scent... He went across the beds of pinks, whose keen perfume came sharply across the rocking, heavy scent of the lilies, and stood alongside the white barrier of flowers. They flagged all loose, as if they were panting. The scent made him drunk.

D. H. Lawrence, *Sons and Lovers*

Trees

I think that I shall never see
A poem as lovely as a tree.

A tree whose hungry mouth is pressed
Against the earth's sweet flowing breast;

A tree that looks at God all day,
And lifts her leafy arms to pray;

A tree that may in summer wear
A nest of robins in her hair;

Upon whose bosom snow has lain;
Who intimately lives with rain.

Poems are made by fools like me,
But only God can make a tree.

Joyce Kilmer

from Night and Day

Till at last the day begins
In the east a-breaking,
In the hedges and the whins
Sleeping birds a-waking.

In the darkness shapes of things,
Houses, trees and hedges,
Clearer grow; and sparrow's wings
Beat on window ledges.

These shall wake the yawning maid;
She the door shall open –
Finding dew on garden glade
And the morning broken.

There my garden grows again
Green and rosy painted,
As at eve behind the pane
From my eyes it fainted.

Just as it was shut away,
Toy-like in the even,
Here I see it glow with day
Under glowing heaven.

Every path and every plot,
Every bush of roses,
Every blue forget-me-not
Where the dew reposes.

Robert Louis Stevenson

The garden is never dead;
growth is always going on,
and growth that can be seen,
and seen with delight.

Henry Ellacombe,
In My Vicarage Garden

Mr Collins invited them to take a stroll in the garden, which was large and well laid out, and to the cultivation of which he attended himself. To work in his garden was one of his most respectable pleasures... Here, leading the way through every walk and cross walk, and scarcely allowing them an interval to utter the praises he asked for, every view was pointed out with a minuteness which left beauty entirely behind.

Jane Austen, *Pride and Prejudice*

The Garden Seat

Its former green is blue and thin,
And its once firm legs sink in and in,
Soon it will break down unaware,
Soon it will break down unaware.

At night when reddest flowers are black,
Those who once sat thereon come back;
Quite a row of them sitting there,
Quite a row of them sitting there.

With them the seat does not break down,
Nor winter freeze them, nor floods drown.
For they are as light as upper air,
For they are as light as upper air!

Thomas Hardy

There were the smoothest lawns in the world stretching down to the edge of the liquid slowness and making, where the water touched them, a line as even as the rim of a champagne glass... The place was a garden of delight.

Henry James, *English Hours*

from On a Fine Crop of Peas being Spoiled by a Storm

When Morrice views his prostrate peas,
By raging whirlwhinds spread,
He wrings his hands, and in amaze
He sadly shakes his head.

'Is this the fruit of my fond toil,
My joy, my pride, my cheer!
Shall one tempestuous hour thus spoil
The labours of a year!

Oh! what avails, that day to day
I nursed the thriving crop,
And settled with my foot the clay,
And reared the social prop!

Ambition's pride had spurred me on
All gard'ners to excel.
I often called them one by one,
And boastingly would tell,

How I prepared the furrowed ground
And how the grain did sow,
Then challenged all the country round
For such an early blow.

How did their bloom my wishes raise!
What hopes did they afford,
To earn my honoured master's praise,
And crown his cheerful board!'

Poor Morrice, wrapt in sad surprise,
Demands in sober mood,
'Should storms molest a man so wise,
A man so just and good?'

Ah! Morrice, cease thy fruitless moan,
Nor at misfortunes spurn,
Misfortune's not thy lot alone;
Each neighbour hath his turn.

Henry Jones

Outside the castle there was a beautiful garden, in which grew bright red and dark blue flowers, and blossoms like flames of fire; the fruit glittered like gold, and the leaves and stems waved to and fro continually. The earth itself was the finest sand, but blue as the flame of burning sulphur. Over everything lay a peculiar blue radiance, as if it were surrounded by the air from above, through which the blue sky shone, instead of the dark depths of the sea. In calm weather the sun could be seen, looking like a purple flower, with the light streaming from the calyx.

Hans Christian Andersen,
The Little Mermaid

How beautiful a circumstance, the improvement of the flower, from the root up to that crown of its life and labours, that bridal-chamber of its beauty and its two-fold love, the nuptial and the parental – the womb, the cradle, and the nursery of the garden!

Samuel Taylor Coleridge, *Anima Poetae*

Upon a Snail

She goes but softly, but she goeth sure;
She stumbles not, as stronger creatures do;
Her journey's shorter, so she may endure
Better than they which do much farther go.
She makes no noise, but stilly seizeth on
The flower or herb appointed for her food,
The which she quietly doth feed upon,
While others range and glare, but find no good.
And though she doth but very softly go,
However 'tis not fast, nor slow, but sure;
And certainly they that do travel so,
The prize they do aim at they do procure.

John Bunyan

When the world wearies, and society ceases to satisfy, there is always the garden.

Minnie Aumônier

Every afternoon, as they were coming from school, the children used to go and play in the Giant's garden.

It was a large lovely garden, with soft green grass. Here and there over the grass stood beautiful flowers like stars, and there were twelve peach-trees that in the springtime broke out into delicate blossoms of pink and pearl, and in the autumn bore rich fruit. The birds sat on the trees and sang so sweetly that the children used to stop their games in order to listen to them. 'How happy we are here!' they cried to each other.

Oscar Wilde, 'The Selfish Giant' in *The Happy Prince and Other Tales*

I don't remember any time quite so perfect since the days when I was too little to do lessons and was turned out with sugar on my eleven o'clock bread and butter on to a lawn closely strewn with dandelions and daisies. The sugar on the bread and butter has lost its charm, but I love the dandelions and daisies even more passionately now than then, and never would endure to see them all mown away if I were not certain that in a day or two they would be pushing up their little faces again as jauntily as ever. During those six weeks I lived in a world of dandelions and delights. The dandelions carpeted the three lawns – they used to be lawns, but have long since blossomed out into meadows filled with every sort of pretty weed, – and under and among the groups of leafless oaks and beeches were blue hepaticas, white anemones, violets, and celandines in sheets. The celandines in particular delighted me with their clean, happy brightness, so beautifully trim and newly varnished, as though they too had had the painters at work on them. Then, when the anemones went, came a few stray periwinkles and Solomon's Seal, and all the birdcherries blossomed in a burst. And then, before I had a little got used to the joy of their flowers against the sky, came the lilacs – masses and masses of them, in clumps on the grass, with other shrubs and trees by the side of walks, and one great continuous bank of them half a mile long right past the west front of the house, away down as far as one could see, shining glorious against a background of firs. When that time came, and when, before it was over, the acacias all blossomed too, and four great clumps of pale, silvery-pink peonies flowered under the south windows, I felt so absolutely happy, and blest, and thankful, and grateful, that I really cannot describe it. My days seemed to melt away in a dream of pink and purple peace.

Elizabeth von Arnim,
Elizabeth and her German Garden

Flowers have an expression of countenance as much as men or animals. Some seem to smile; some have a sad expression; some are pensive and diffident; others again are plain, honest and upright, like the broad-faced sunflower and the hollyhock.

Henry Ward Beecher

from The Planting of the Apple-Tree

Come, let us plant the apple-tree.
Cleave the tough greensward with
the spade;
Wide let its hollow bed be made;
There gently lay the roots, and there
Sift the dark mould with kindly care,
And press it o'er them tenderly,
As, round the sleeping infant's feet,
We softly fold the cradle-sheet;
So plant we the apple-tree.

What plant we in this apple-tree?
Buds, which the breath of summer days
Shall lengthen into leafy sprays;

Boughs where the thrush, with
crimson breast,
Shall haunt and sing and hide her nest;
We plant, upon the sunny lea,
A shadow for the noontide hour,
A shelter from the summer shower,
When we plant the apple-tree.

What plant we in this apple-tree?
Sweets for a hundred flowery springs
To load the May-wind's restless wings,
When, from the orchard row, he pours
Its fragrance through our open doors;
A world of blossoms for the bee,
Flowers for the sick girl's silent room,
For the glad infant sprigs of bloom,
We plant with the apple-tree.

What plant we in this apple-tree?
Fruits that shall swell in sunny June,
And redden in the August noon,
And drop, when gentle airs come by,
That fan the blue September sky,
While children come, with cries of glee,
And seek them where the fragrant grass
Betrays their bed to those who pass,
At the foot of the apple-tree.

William Cullen Bryant

Large or small, the garden should look both orderly and rich. It should be well fenced from the outer world. It should by no means imitate either the wilfulness or the wildness of Nature, but should look like a thing never seen except near a house.

William Morris,
Hopes and Fears for Art

I used to visit and revisit it a dozen times a day, and stand in deep contemplation over my vegetable progeny with a love that nobody could share or conceive of who had never taken part in the process of creation. It was one of the most bewitching sights in the world to observe a hill of beans thrusting aside the soil, or rows of early peas just peeping forth sufficiently to trace a line of delicate green.

Nathaniel Hawthorne,
Mosses from an Old Manse

Being thus prepared for us in all ways, and made beautiful, and good for food, and for building, and for instruments of our hands, this race of plants, deserving boundless affection and admiration from us, becomes, in proportion to their obtaining it, a nearly perfect test of our being in right temper of mind and way of life; so that no one can be far wrong in either who loves trees enough, and everyone is assuredly wrong in both who does not love them, if his life has brought them in his way.

John Ruskin, *Modern Painters*

The Blackbird

O blackbird! Sing me something well:
While all the neighbours shoot thee round,
I keep smooth plats of fruitful ground,
Where thou may'st warble, eat and dwell.

The espaliers and the standards all
Are thine; the range of lawn and park:
The unnetted black-hearts ripen dark,
All thine, against the garden wall.

Yet, tho' I spared thee all the spring,
Thy sole delight is, sitting still,
With that gold dagger of thy bill
To fret the summer jenneting.

A golden bill! the silver tongue,
　　Cold February loved, is dry:
　　Plenty corrupts the melody
That made thee famous once, when young:

　　And in the sultry garden-squares,
Now thy flute-notes are changed to coarse,
　　I hear thee not at all, or hoarse
　　As when a hawker hawks his wares.

　　Take warning! he that will not sing
　　While yon sun prospers in the blue,
　　Shall sing for want, ere leaves are new,
Caught in the frozen palms of Spring.

Alfred, Lord Tennyson

I think the true gardener is a lover of his flowers, not a critic of them. I think the true gardener is the reverent servant of Nature, not her truculent, wife-beating master. I think the true gardener, the older he grows, should more and more develop a humble, grateful and uncertain spirit.

Reginald Farrer, *In a Yorkshire Garden*

My greenhouse is never so pleasant as when we are just on the point of being turned out of it. The gentleness of the autumnal suns, and the calmness of this latter season, make it a much more agreeable retreat than we ever find it in summer... I sit with all the windows and door wide open, and am regaled with the scent of every flower in a garden as full of flowers as I have known how to make it.

William Cowper to Rev John Newton, 18 September 1784

Hence we went to Swallowfield; this house is after the ancient building of honourable gentlemen's houses, when they kept up ancient hospitality, but the gardens and waters as elegant as 'tis possible to make a flat, by art and industry, and no mean expense, my lady being so extraordinarily skilled in the flowery part, and my lord in diligence of planting; so that I have hardly seen a seat which shows more tokens of it than what is to be found here, not only in the delicious and rarest fruits of a garden, but in those innumerable timber trees in the ground about the seat, to the greatest ornament and benefit of the place. There is one orchard of 1000 golden, and other cider pippins; walks and groves of elms, limes, oaks, and other trees. The garden is so beset with all manners of sweet shrubs, that it perfumes the air.

The distribution also of the quarters, walks, and parterres, is excellent. The nurseries, kitchen garden full of the most desirable plants; two very noble Orangeries well furnished; but above all, the canal and fishponds, the one fed with a white, the other with a black running water, fed by a quick and swift river, so well and plentifully stored with fish, that for pike, carp, bream and tench, I never saw anything approaching it.

John Evelyn, *Evelyn's Diary*

from The Glory of the Garden

Our England is a garden that is full of
stately views,
Of borders, beds and shrubberies and
lawns and avenues,
With statues on the terraces and peacocks
strutting by;
But the Glory of the Garden lies in more
than meets the eye.

[...]

Our England is a garden, and such gardens
are not made
By singing: – 'Oh, how beautiful!' and
sitting in the shade,
While better men than we go out and start
their working lives
At grubbing weeds from gravel-paths with
broken dinner-knives.

Rudyard Kipling

An October Garden

In my Autumn garden I was fain
To mourn among my scattered roses;
Alas for that last rosebud that uncloses
To Autumn's languid sun and rain
When all the world is on the wane!
Which has not felt the sweet constraint
of June,
Nor heard the nightingale in tune.

Broad-faced asters by my garden walk,
You are but coarse compared with roses:
More choice, more dear that rosebud
which uncloses,
Faint-scented, pinched, upon its stalk,
That least and last which cold winds balk;
A rose it is though least and last of all,
A rose to me though at the fall.

Christina Rossetti

If you're interested in finding out more about our books, find us on Facebook at **Summersdale Publishers** and follow us on Twitter at **@Summersdale**.

www.summersdale.com